This Present Judgment

Why Do I Go Through So Much Hell When I Know That I Am a Child of God?

By: TeRaze Mickle

Author Bio

Dr. TeRaze Mickle, co-founder of Mickle Publishers, is a pastor, educator, and theologian whose ministry and scholarship have inspired believers for more than two decades. A graduate of Southern University and Texas Bible Institute & Seminary, she holds a Master's Degree in Education and a Doctorate in Divinity. Alongside her husband, Dr. Toby Mickle, she continues to serve as a pastor and spiritual counselor devoted to empowering lives through faith and practical wisdom.

Her landmark work, This Present Judgement: Why Do I Go Through So Much Hell When I Know That I Am a Child of God?-originally copyright in 2001 with a foreword by Bishop Carlton Pearson-returns in this new edition with contemporary reflections and teachings that speak to today's generation. A companion volume, This Present Judgement II, is forthcoming, continuing her life-affirming message of endurance, deliverance, and divine purpose.

Copyright © 2001 by TeRaze Mickle

Paperback ISBN: 978-0-9709977-6-0

All rights reserved.

No part of this book may be reproduced, stored in a retrieval system, or transmitted in any form or by any means—electronic, mechanical, photocopying, recording, or otherwise—without prior written permission from the publisher, except for brief quotations in reviews or scholarly works.

Published by **Mickle Publishers**

Dallas-Fort Worth, Texas

Unless otherwise indicated, all Scripture quotations are from the **King James Version** of the Bible. Public domain. This book is a work of biblical teaching and personal interpretation. It is not intended to provide legal, medical, or psychological advice. Readers should consult appropriate professionals where necessary.

Printed in the United States of America

Second Edition

To God Be The Glory
Who is continually at work in me …

Special Thanks …
To my loving husband, Pastor Toby Mickle, whose continued in-
spiration and encouragement made this book possible.

To my son, Toby Mickle, Jr., who labored in the design of the
cover and assisted in the transcription.

To my daughter, DeZerai Mickle, who discerned that mom just
needed peace and quiet.

To my mom, Barbara Stamps, who supports and encourages me in
all I put my hands to do.

Thanks Editors
To Rita Bynum, my maid of honor, my son's godmother, and a woman
of God.

To Shonda Little, who co-pastors with her husband, Robert Little,
at Agape Fellowship of Davant, Louisiana.

To Pastor Nathaniel and Patricia Jones over
Restoring Lives
Ministry in Bartlesville, Oklahoma.

TABLE OF CONTENTS

Introduction

Chapter One:

    The Church

Chapter Two:
    The Time Has Come

Chapter Three:
    Why Judgment?

Chapter Four:
    The Trial

Chapter Five:

Duration of the Trial

Chapter Six:
    Testimonials

Chapter Seven:
The Verdict

INTRODUCTION

In Matthew 10:34-36 Jesus said:

> Do not think that I am come to bring peace on
> earth: I came not to send peace, but a sword.
>
> For I come to set a man at variance against his
> father, and the daughter against her mother, and
> the daughter in law against her mother in law,
>
> And a man's foes shall be they of his own house-
> hold.

Well, this is sort of what I want to do – let the worms out of the can. I want to talk about something that's uncomfortable – **JUDGMENT**. Judgment for the believer is nothing to dread or fear. It is vital.

Many believers think that if there is no peace, God cannot be in it. Nonetheless, Jesua said it plainly that he came **not** to bring peace.

Matthew 23:23 says:

Woe to you, scribes and Pharisees, hypocrites!
For you pay tithe of mint and anise and cumin,
and have neglected the weightier matters of the
law; judgment, mercy, and faith. These should
you have done without leaving the others undone.

I've read books about the faith of God, the mercy of God, and even the end time judgment but none about this present judgment. We under-stand that judgment has a place, a season in the life of every be-liever. It comes to bring death but in the end life. Judgment kills selfish ambitions, wrong motives, pride, false humility, traditions of men, idolatry, that comparative spirit and more. Like the Apostle Paul, we too must die daily. Judgment answers the question …. Why? Why do the righteous suffer? Why does God permit tragedy?

Psalm 50: 4-6 says:

> He shall call the heavens from above, and to
>> the earth that He may judge his people.
>
> Gather my saints together unto me those that
>> have made a covenant with me by sacrifice.
>
> And the heavens shall declare his righteousness:
>> for God is judge himself.

The Lord says to gather the people who have made a covenant with him – the saints. Why? He is gathering his people that he may judge them. Yes, God himself is the judge. **We have known Him as Jehovah Jireh, our provider, but we have not known him as JUDGE.** I believe that there is something in this book for every believer. Many know the works of God but few know his ways, the reasoning of God. Judgment has always been the way of God.

> Deuteronomy 32:4
>
> **… all the ways of God are judgment.**

My purpose in writing this book is that it would illuminate, clarify and comfort all who read it.

Chapter 1

THE CHURCH

At the end of 1994, I uncannily began to weep. While weeping, I began inwardly to inquire of the Lord as to why I was endowed with a spirit of intercession? He replied,

> *"The state of the church affects the nations"*.

Shortly before this, I remember asking the Lord, what in the world was going on? There were young Christian men and women dying all around me and it bothered me. It seemed as if many of them had died prematurely. I wasn't really expecting God to respond, so when He did, I thought, what does that mean? I began to pray more earnestly inquiring of the Lord concerning his response to me. I didn't really understand! Then, shortly after, I understood.

The Lord was showing me that He was about to groom his church. He was about to change the state of the church. He was about to change the characterization, the attributes of the church. Yes, He was about to groom his people for distinction and purpose.

The state of the nation pivots on the state of the church. Our homes, businesses, and all facets of life are affected. I believe that God is shaking us to awaken us to positively affect our nation. Indeed, this was a very alarming and awakening time for me as I endeavored to know the state of the church.

When God's about to do something that affects the nation, He first reveals it in natural things and then spiritual. When the seasons are about to change, there are signs that indicate this change. Autumn is a season of reflection. It is a time to summarize past activities and to gain insight into future achievements. Following autumn is winter, a season of barrenness. The season of the church at large was about to change from autumn to winter.

Genesis 1:14 says:

And God said, Let there be lights in the firma-

> ment of heaven to divide the day from the night;
> and let them be for signs, and for seasons, and
> for days, and years:

The two lights here refer to the sun and the moon. They indicate signs, seasons, days, and years. Men have always watched the sun for signs of the passing seasons. The change in seasons is caused by the changing position of the earth relative to the sun. The word "season" here does not refer to a season of the year such as autumn, but it indicates an appointed or set time. Nonetheless, at the time of my experience, the season was changing from autumn to winter – first the natural then the spiritual.

The Book of Matthew, chapter 24, depicts signs of the end time judgment. My belief is that this present judgment is a shadow or foretaste of the final judgment. Therefore, I had expected to see some of these same signs but to a lesser degree. On November 3, 1994, there was a sign in the sky – a total eclipse occurred in South America. A total solar eclipse takes place when the sun appears dark as the moon passes between the sun and the earth. Notable earthquakes in various areas also occurred. Particularly, on November 14,

1994, there was an earthquake in Mindoro Philippines that registered a moment of 7.1 on the Richter scale. There were signs all around me, but I didn't see the flag waiving – I didn't hear the alarm ringing. It wasn't until young Christians my own age began to die that I was awaken. Some may say that this means nothing. However, I'm one who believes that nothing happens by chance. *If events just happened by chance, then God would by no means now or ever be in control.* Selah!

The Church's Responsibility

II Chronicles 7:14 says:

If my people, which are called by my name shall
humble themselves, and pray and seek my face,
and turn from their wicked ways; then will I hear
from heaven and will forgive their sin, and heal
their land.

This passage of scripture indicates the necessity of the church's role in our nation. We must humble ourselves, pray, seek the face of God, and turn from our wicked ways before we can truly be the voice of God. ***We are not truly the voice of God until we are the people He's called us to be.*** In this passage, God is not talking to the world but to church folk. We would like to think that he is talking to the prostitute, the pimp, the drug dealer, the drug user, etc… But, the truth of the matter is that He is talking to us about our sin, about our wicked ways.

We, the body of Christ, must come to the understanding that we have an awesome responsibility. We are placed on this earth to establish the rule of God's kingdom. Anything that illegally transpires in the earth is the fault or negligence of the church. We need to speak and act when it is required of us. If God has raised us up, it is not to sit silently in the comfort zone. We are to stand in unity as the church of the Lord Jesus Christ. I'm not just talking about the five-fold ministry but to each member in particular. We must all do our part. No part or member is insignificant. <u>God is not waiting on the **world** to get right, He is waiting on the **church.**</u> The reality is that when we humble ourselves, pray, seek, and turn, God will hear from heaven, forgive our sins, and heal our land.

The State of the Church

I see the church in an immature state. We think that the things that have come against us are the plan of the adversary, but it is God at work in us. We have to arrive at the place where nothing shakes or moves us from the path of righteousness. It has to be said of the church, as it was said of JESUS, "we changeth not". **The church will triumph, but the process of judgment must take place in us.** The church as we know it will not remain. No, it shall be changed. Some maybe saying, well, what are you saying sister TeRaze? I'm saying that we have been confessing Christ as Lord but now He is about to be formed in us. Many of us have been yearning for what we know not and I believe that this is it. We are tired of church as usual. It isn't what or the way we expected, but this is it. **Yes, the time is at hand; judgment is upon us.** The church has not begun to reflect the true Jesus. Unless judgment takes place, we cannot become the glorious bride foretold in the scriptures. Jesus had many thoughts concerning his church.

Ephesians 5:26-27 states:

>   That he might sanctify and cleanse it with the
>   washing of the word,
>
>   That he might present it to himself a glorious
>   church, without spot, or wrinkle, holy, and with-
>   out blemish.

The desire of the Lord is that she, the Church, be holy and without blemish having no spot or wrinkle. While pondering this passage these four words stood out - spot, wrinkle, blemish, holy.

Spots

Spots are defined as those defects in our character, our short-comings, those things that would cause shame or embarrassment. In these last years, we've heard and seen things in the media that has brought reproach to the name of Christ. The sacrifices of old had to be presented without spots. Romans 12: 1 admonishes us to present our bodies as living sacrifices holy and acceptable unto God. Just as one washes clothes, the Lord desires to wash us with the word to remove the spots.

I'm not just talking about spots we can see but also those spots that we have not detected - blind spots. In regard to the eyes, a blind spot is determined by testing. It's the same with spiritual spots. God allows persecution and trials to test us while we are here on the earth. I know this is a strange thing to say, but I'm glad God does it this way. If He had only allowed me to see those defects on Judgment Day, I'd have to say that God was unjust.

Job 11: 14- 15 reads:

If inquity be in thine hand, put it far away,
and let no wickedness dwell in thy tabernacles.

For then shalt thou lift up thy face without spot;

In the Book of Job, Zophar, one of Job's friends, declares a unique thing. He says that the putting away of iniquity or wickedness is to be without spots. This is something to think about since the Lord said that his people must turn from their wicked ways. We, the people of God, have wicked ways that we need to turn away from.

Wrinkles

Job 16:8 says:

And thou hast filled me with wrinkles, which is
   a witness against me:

Brother Job defines wrinkles as that which testifies or witnesses against us. It's interesting to note that heat or steam gets the wrinkles out. When God allows the heat to be turned up through persecutions, sufferings, and trials of various sorts, it is to iron out the wrinkles.

Blemishes

Blemishes are our faults. Our Lord wants to present us faultless before the throne. The Book of Jude verse 24 declares that the **only** one able to do so. The sacrifices of old had to be without blemish. Remember, the Bible declares that no fault was found in the Lamb of God.

Be Holy

I Peter 1:15-16 says:

> But as he which hath called you is holy in all,
> so be ye holy in all manner of conversation;
>
> Because it is written, be ye holy; for I am holy.

In the last years, the word "holy" has literally come alive to me. The word "holy" means to be consecrated or set apart for the service of God. I've always had a desire to live right and to do the right thing, but I had no understanding of how it could be done. It was by the grace of God that I was kept. Graciously, by seeking the face of God, I have discovered some precious truths. I now know that apart from God, we cannot be holy; it is He who empowers us to live holy. To live holy one must have power over that which keeps us from being holy – sin. Holiness simply means that we have power over sin. In other words, we don't have to sin. I must admit that it is shocking to discover that a great number of believers don't believe this. Nonetheless, the scriptures bear witness that we **can** live above sin. For years I've sang songs about seeing Jesus, not realizing that one of the requirements to meet Him is that I be holy. Hebrews 12:14 tells us that without holiness no man shall see God.

When I was growing up, holiness meant wearing a long white dress, head covered, and no make-up. Oh, but when you've partaken of the sufferings of Christ, this scripture takes on a whole different meaning. You no longer just toil concerning the outward man, but you labor to make the inward man radiant.
The Lord is actually at work in us. He is preparing a bride. The Lord desires a bride that will remain, not change, through the good times and the bad times; one that will endure.

Chapter 2

THE TIME HAS COME

The last years of my life have felt like pure hell. It has consisted of manifold trials. Everything I thought I had accomplished had been stripped away. In great anguish, I sought the Lord concerning my troubles. I felt like I was in a season where God had removed His hand of grace. I toiled many days and nights praying, studying, pondering my ways, my actions, trying to unfold why it seemed like God had left me. Yes, I felt like God had forsaken me!

I had resigned from an excellent paying job, sold my dream house, and more all in submission and obedience to the plan of God. My desire had been to be in the perfect will of God and not just his permissive will for my life. I expected my life to be exceedingly better since I had obeyed God in these great matters. However, it didn't happen that way. As a matter of fact, one of the first things I remember was quite the contrast; the Lord became silent. I had experienced dry seasons in my life before, but nothing like this. I had once felt close to God, but now He was silent. Others shared words with me, but I needed to hear directly from Him, one-on-one, face-to-face. Then, one day our sovereign Lord began to disclose His way to me. The scripture he spoke to me was I Peter 4:17. This wasn't one of my favorite scriptures that I had memorized so I had to look it up and it reads as follows:

> **For the time is come that judgment must began at the house of God: and if it first began at us, what shall the end be of them that obey not the gospel of God?**

When I began reading this, I literally threw my Bible down. I didn't want to hear anything about judgment, although later I was forced to face it. Because of my troubles, I had already entertained the thought that I might be under judgment by God or even cursed. The only judgment I had ever heard of was the Great White Throne Judgment, the final judgment. In this passage, we see that according to God's calendar, it is time for something. And, that something is the judgment of the House of God. Notice Peter said that the time has come not that it will come. In other words, **this is not something in the future but the present, the now.** When Jesus was in the Garden Of Gethsemane, he said, "The hour has come". Jesus had to drink of the cup of suffering and so do we. Naturally, this stirred another question in me. Was there more than one judgment? Yes. I have come to believe that there is more than one judgment. The type of judgment we will talk about in this book is a type of pruning judgment. Its' purpose is to prune, to expiate. Actually, in plants there are two types of pruning, corrective and maintenance. Corrective pruning is the process of chastening; its purpose is to punish in order to correct. Maintenance pruning is the upkeep. It is to keep us on the right path and to mold us into all God has called us to be. However, whether it is maintenance or corrective pruning, the execution of them both feels the same. Maintenance pruning is the type of judgment that will be discussed in this book. This judgment deals with our response to God and man while upon the earth.

Now Judgment

The passage John 9:39 had boggled my mind but now required my attention. For years I blew this scripture off simply because I didn't understand it. And it reads as follow:

For judgment I am come into this world, that they which see not might see, and they which see might be made blind.

If you read this chapter from the beginning, you'll find that it's about a man-child born blind. Then, the disciples asked Jesus, "Who sinned this man or his parents that he was born blind"? Jesus answered them and said, "Neither this man nor his parents sinned, but that the works of God should be revealed in him." It's amazing that most of us still think the same way the disciples did then. <u>We believe that judgment is **always** a result of sin.</u> Of course, some sickness can be a result of sin, but not in this case. Sometimes sickness is permitted because of divine purpose. Jesus said it plainly that this sickness was not a result of sin. I've often wondered what went on with this man. Nonetheless, I'm reminded of Romans 9, the story of the potter and the clay.

<u>Can one say to his maker why has thou made me thus?</u> I believe that this man didn't even care that he was born blind only that now he could see. This scripture still bothered me because I didn't see God's divine plan for this man. Notice, Paul says, "that the works of God might be revealed". Maybe my consolation lay in understanding this. While Jesus was on the earth he said, "Believe me for my works sake". What is it all about? Then, I began to see that the works of God reveal the glory of God. The psalmist said that, "The heavens declare the glory of God". Yes, **the glory of God is revealed through his works.**

What is Judgment?

First of all, let me say this, the purpose for which Christ came to earth to dwell amongst man has everything to do with judgment. It is a startling fact that Christ came into the world for **JUDGMENT, *but he did*.** Isaiah 42: 1-4 depicts the urgency for Christ to deliver judgment in the earth.

Behold, my servant, whom I uphold; mine elect,
in whom my soul delighted; I put my spirit upon

him: he shall bring judgment to the Gentiles.

He shall not cry, nor lift up, nor cause his
voice to be heard in the street.

A bruised reed shall he not break, and the
smoking flax shall he not quench: he shall
bring forth judgment unto truth.

He shall not fail nor be discouraged, till he
have set judgment in the earth: and the isles
shall wait for his law.

<u>*Jesus could not rest until judgment was set in the earth.*</u>
What is judgment? *Judgment is the justice system if God.* <u>It is a divine sentence or decision to try or call in question</u>. God Almighty made the decision to sentence Christ to die for the sins of all mankind and Christ accepted the verdict. Judgment makes a distinction between holy and unholy; clean and unclean; truth and falsehood. Judgment tries the reins of men. Judgment removes the impurities, the unwanted, the ungodly things. Just like

the man born blind, **judgment causes us to awaken spiritually; it causes us to see.**

II Thessalonians 1:4-5 reads:

> So that we ourselves boast of you among the
> churches of God for your patience and faith
> in all of your persecutions and tribulations
> that you endure.
>
> Which is manifest evidence of the righteous
> judgment of God, that you may be counted worthy
> of the kingdom of God, for which you also suffer;

First of all, I want you to notice that Paul calls it **"righteous judgment."** Secondly, I want you to notice that **something extraordinary takes place.** Paul says we **boast** about your perseverance and faith in all your persecutions and trials. When have we, the church at large, praised those who have preserved through manifold trials? No, we are quick to say, "All they need

is a little more faith or they must not be walking with God." The Apostle Paul says that we have been **boosting about you**. And, the rewards for persevering is that now you are counted worthy of the kingdom. Hallelujah!

Trials and persecutions are integral parts of the judgment process. The fact that these saints are withstanding is the manifest evidence that God is with them.

<u>Now, let me tell you what judgment is not.</u> Jeremiah 10:24 reads

> **O Lord, correct me; but with judgment; not thine anger, lest thou bring me to nothing.**

In this passage, we see a distinction between judgment and anger. **Judgment is for correction**. Jeremiah says that he'd rather be corrected by judgment and not anger. *Judgment to the believer is not the anger of God but God's mercy toward man.*

Unregenerate man cannot perceive this fact. Sometimes the thing we fight the most is what is best for us. There have been many who didn't make it through the same trial you just overcame. Many shot their brains out because they were without God. The fact that you are still here and in your right mind is evidence that God is with you.

Discerning Judgment

Many Christians do not discern judgment. The word "discern" means to distinguish, to perceive. It also means to hear, to give ear to, to consider. Let me state clearly that only those who seek the Lord can continuously discern judgment.

Ecclesiastes 8:5-6 reads:

Whoso keepeth the commandment shall feel no
evil thing; and the wise in heart discerneth
both time and judgment.

Because to every purpose there is time and
judgment, therefore the misery of man is great
upon him.

Solomon says that a wise man's heart discerneth two things: *time and judgment.* The wise heart discerneth not the foolish heart. Verse 6 tells us that every purpose is affected by both **time and judgment.** Now get hold of the last portion of the verse. <u>It states that we are miserable, filled with anger, because we do not understand time and judgment.</u> *A lot of our frustration in trying to do the will of God stem from not discerning these two factors.* <u>The reason why we ask the "When Lord?" questions is because we don't understand time. When will it come to pass? The reason we ask the "Why Lord?" questions is because we don't understand judgment. Why did this happen Lord?</u> This verse just pricks at my heart. We who desire to know God must begin to discern these two things. Too often we say that something is God when it is not, and vice versa, simply because we don't discern both time and judgment. Let's view I Kings 3: 9-11.

    Give therefore thy servant an understanding heart
        to judge thy people, good and bad: for who is able
            to judge this thy so great a people.

    And the speech pleased the Lord, that Solomon
        had asked this thing.

> And God said unto him, because thou hast asked this thing, and hast not asked for thyself, long life, riches for thyself, nor asked for thy life of thine enemies; but hast asked for thyself understanding to discern judgment.

Of course, I've read this before, but I've never felt the magnitude of it; this is powerful! I had to check my heart after reading this. What would I have asked for? God said that he was pleased with his request. Solomon asked for an understanding heart to know judgment. The word "discern" in verse 11 means to hear. You see, judgment comes from the mouth of God. Saints, we have been asking for the wrong things. We haven't had the heart of God and consequently we haven't had a heart for His people.

Now, how do we discern judgment? Well, the simplest way that I can explain it is that it comes from the mouth of God; you have to **HEAR** it. God Almighty declares it. Each time I would seek the Lord, I would hear Him say, "My hand is stretched out still". I thought something overwhelmingly glorious was about to transpire in my life, but instead there were false accusations, death to my business, attacks on my physical body, and financial struggles. Again, every time I went in prayer, the Lord was still saying," My hand was stretched out still". Then, I began to search the scriptures. Every time the Lord said those words, it was when judgment was upon a people or when his wrath was released upon a people. Then, I began to see the picture. I was the accused in the courtroom. I was the one being tried. I was the one that Satan was trying to disprove. It was my time to take up my cross and bear it. It took time for me to rend my heart and to say, "Thine will be done", but I came to the realization that God had allowed some things for purpose. <u>He revealed some character flaws for purpose</u> – that I may be more like Him. In order to go into deeper depths and higher heights with God, I had to lay aside all weights and wicked ways in me. <u>My troubles did not come to set me back, but to bring me into new dimensions in God.</u>

Judgment Loosed

When I decided that no matter what the cost I would surrender totally to God, all hell broke loose. Not only was I "going through" but countless others were "going through." My belief was that our troubles were due to the fact that God had loosed judgment in the land. Yes, I did say that God had loosed judgment in the land. Of course we had experienced trials before, but nothing like this. Nothing seemed to lift because judgment had been loosed from the heavens. Everything has a set time and I believe that it was and is the set time for the judgment of the church. Isaiah 54:17 reads:

No weapon that is formed against thee shall prosper; and every tongue that shall rise against thee in judgment thou shall condemn.

The Bible clearly states that the weapons will be formed against us, but the end result is that it shall not prosper. Now, let's look at this scripture again and I want you to notice the time when tongues will rise

up against you. The time when tongues rise up against you is **the time of judgment**. Now, let's look back and see when judgment was loosed in the earth.
<u>Judgment was loosed in the earth after the resurrection of Christ.</u>

John 12:31 says:

> **Now** is the judgment of this world; now the ruler
> of the world will be cast out.

You see most of us thought that there was only the end time judgment. Revelation 12:12 warns us of the judgment to come for it says, "Woe to the inhabitants of the earth". When Satan was cast out, the heavens rejoiced while great wrath fell upon the earth. Yes, this present judgment began.

The Book of Job is an account of a man under judgment. Many of us are familiar with the sufferings of Job, but would not classify it as judgment. Before I began to study this, I thought that the books of the Bible were written in the chronological order in which they were placed in the Bible. However, some historians place the book of Job between the time of Abraham and Moses. If this is true, maybe there is something here that God wanted us to know right from the beginning. We think of judgment as a negative thing, but that is not always true. Even in a court of law, judgment can be for as well as against.

Job 40: 8 reads:

Will thou annul My judgment? Wilt thou condemn
me, that thou mayest be righteous?

God said to Job, would you indeed annul My judgment? Yes, God Himself spoke to Job and said his troubles were because of His judgment, His decision; a decision God Almighty made. And, it could not have been judgment against Job 1:1 & Job 2:10. These passages denote Job to be a man who eschewed evil and who in the time of trouble did not sin against God with his mouth. Also, Job 2:3 states that Job was destroyed without cause. Therefore, this judgment had to be **FOR** and not *against* Job.

Elihu, one of the three friends of Job, states in Job 36:17 that Job was filled with the judgment of the wicked. Elihu didn't realize that there was a judgment due to righteous; he judged Job wrongfully.

The Lord told Peter that Satan desired to sift him as wheat but he had prayed for him that his faith fail not. The word "sift" means to "riddle". The word "riddle" means to "sift", to separate, to puncture through, to find a flaw in, to criticize and disprove. Now I ask the question, was Peter sifted? Of course he was. So, what can we conclude? We can conclude that God gave Satan permission to sift Peter. And, I might also add that God has given Satan permission to disprove you.

The accusations will not cease until we are with the Lord. So, we must remember the words of Jesus, "Be of good cheer for I have overcome the world".

Now, I know someone is asking this question. Is it God who performs these evil acts? The answer is, of course, no, but God does allow it. I believe that God allows Satan to attack us for he knows that if we continue to trust him, we will win.

II Peter 2:9 says:

The Lord knows how to deliver the righteous out of their troubles.

I use to think that if God only knew surely he would deliver me at once. But, now I see that He knows that this circumstance, this trouble, this situation is going to build in me His character, His nature; He sees that my end will be good. When Jesus was in the Garden of Gethsemane, he said, "He could have sent ten thousand angels." You see, God is able to deliver us at any time. He sees exactly what's going on in our lives.

Whom Does Judgment Affect?

I've toiled many hours with this one question. Whom does judgment affect? I've come to the conclusion that if I'm under judgment, it not only affects me but all in relation with me. Let's consider this scenario: A male, married with three children, is sentenced, whether justly or unjustly, to five years in prison. Now, I ask you, who is affected? Judgment affects all. And having said that let me add this: **Regardless of whether the sentence was just or unjust, all will experience judgment.** Most people think that judgment is only the result of sin or some unlawful deed - not so. Judgment is going to take place regardless. You see, I've come to realize that judgment, **righteous judgment**, is and has always been God's way of dealing with his people.

How Does Judgment Begin?

Now, I know that I am not the only one to ask this question. How does judgment began or rather how do you know that judgment is upon you? It took me a while to see this, but I finally began to see that judgment begins with death – death to something. Whether it is death to a business, a ministry, a person, etc., death will take place. Think about it – Ananias and Sapphira dropped dead, Uzza dropped dead. Ananias and Sapphire dropped dead because judgment had been loosed in the camp.

Quite often we do not understand God's way of executing His word; nonetheless, we must continue to trust him.

During this time of study, Psalms 9:16 took hold of me and it reads as follows.

The Lord is known by the judgment he executes.

This is a powerful scripture for it said to me that *if I could somehow*

understand judgment, I could understand Him, I could get to know Him. The Apostle Paul cried, "That I may know Him, and the power of his resurrection, and the fellowship of his suffering, being con-formable to his death." No one in their right mind would want to go through suffering, so Paul knows something. Paul came to know that judgment had to take place for him to know the Father. ***There is no way to know the Lord except by judgment.***

Chapter 3

WHY JUDGMENT?

> Of the increase of his government and peace
> there shall be no end, upon the throne of
> David, and upon his kingdom, to order it, and
> to establish it with judgment and with justice
> from henceforth even forever, the zeal of the
> Lord of hosts will perform this.

This scripture, found in Isaiah 9:7, tells us something about the government of God. Government here is the empire of God. It refers to the rule, the dominion, or system of God. It is God's way of doing things. What I want you to notice here is that **the kingdom of God is <u>established</u> by judgment and justice. The foundation of the kingdom is laid by judgment.** Oh, judgment has to come!

I Chronicles 13: 9-10 gives an account of how God made a breach on Uzza for touching the ark. A breach is the term used when one fails to observe the law. The law stated that no one shall touch any holy thing lest they die. Until now I never understood why God was so wroth. Laws are established by first decreeing them and then enforcing them. Uzza didn't adhere to the government of God. Every kingdom is governed by laws. God had to enforce the law; it was all about government. Without government, the kingdom would be chaotic and void of order. **Unless judgment takes place, the kingdom cannot be established.**

Isaiah 9:6 says:

For unto us a child is born, unto us a son
is given: and the government shall be upon
his shoulder…

"And the government shall be upon his shoulder." The shoulder is figuratively the region or place where burdens are carried. Similarly, the ark was to be carried upon the shoulder.

Let's take it a step further and read Psalms 97:2:

Clouds and darkness are round about him: righteous-

ness and judgment are the habitation of his throne.

The throne of God, the place where God lives is established by righteousness and judgment. God's kingdom on the earth is founded in the same manner as the heavenly kingdom – **righteousness and judgment.**

The kingdom shall be ordered *or set in order by judgment and justice.* Judgment came to King Hezekiah because his house was out of order. Judgment came to give structure; to align his house to the will of God. I believe in my own life that I was doing the right things but out of order. There is a certain way that things are done in the kingdom and we need to search out the order of God. *Unless judgment takes place, order cannot be established in the kingdom.*

As I pondered the establishment of the kingdom, I began to wonder what the kingdom of God was like. Luke 13: 18-19 reads:

Then said he, unto what is the kingdom of God like? And where unto shall I resemble it?

>It is a grain of mustard seed, which a man took
>>and hide in a field, and it grew, and waxed a
>>>great tree; and the fowls of the air lodged in
>>>>the branches of it.

The kingdom of God starts in seed form and develops into a tree. Psalms 1 tells us that we are like trees planted by the rivers of water that bringeth forth fruit in their season. John 15: 1 and 2 reads:

>I am the vine, and my Father is the husbandman.

>Every branch in Me that does not bear fruit he
>>taketh away: and every branch that beareth fruit,
>>>he prunes that it may bear more fruit.

Judgment comes to bring forth fruit. If the church at large does not produce fruit, how does the world see us? Can we effectively reach our nation? Matthew 7:16 says that we are known by the fruit we bear.

In this parable, Jesus describes himself as the vine and those who have become his disciples as the branches. If we remain attached to Him, the source, we will produce fruit. The Lord judges some of the branches fruitless and others fruitful. The unfruitful branches are taken away while the fruitful branches are sentenced to be pruned.

    The word "prune" means to cutback parts for better shape or more fruitful growth. A plant is pruned for the same purpose as people, to get more out of it; to enhance its ornamental value and to fulfill the purpose for which it was chosen. Notice in John 15:2 that only the branches that were bearing fruit were pruned. The pruning process is painful because it cuts away what is unwanted. The Father is glorified when we bear much fruit. His intent is that our fruit remain. We do not want to be like the fig tree that Christ cut off. Plants are young trees and must be pruned continuously to ensure good fruit. A good tree cannot bring forth evil fruit.

    John 15:16 tells us that Christ ordained us to bring forth. A good tree cannot bring forth evil fruit. The word "ordain" here means to prepare, to place, or set forth. The bearing of the fruit is mentioned in Galations 5:22-23 - love, joy, peace, patience, kindness, goodness, faithfulness, gentleness, self control. The Full Life Study Bible states that **the fruit is the quality of Christian character that Christ wants to bring to maturity in our lives.** The fruit of the Spirit is contrast to the deeds of the sinful nature. Fruit is produced in us when we learn to obey the Spirit's unction.

Producing Fruit

John 12:24 says:

> **Verify, verify, I say unto you, except a corn of wheat fall into the ground and die, it abideth alone. But if it die, it bringeth forth much fruit.**

From this passage, we can see that *if we don't allow the dying process, the suffering, we cannot produce fruit.* The seed has to go into the ground to get rooted. If we could see in the ground, we could see how gravity pulls the roots downward where it finds water. Then, of course, the water and the light cause the seed to grow. We have to die. Or in other words, it is imperative that judgment come. **Judgment** *sentences us to die that we may bring forth more fruit.*

Other Bible translations us the word "purge" instead of "prune". You see, *judgment comes to purge.* Isaiah 4:2-4 depicts an example of the branch that has been purged. The branch here is God's people.

Verse 2 tells us that after the branch has been purged, its fruit shall be excellent. *Excellence in ministry cannot take place without judgment taking place.* Verse 3 tells us that those in Zion, the remnant, shall be holy. Remember, the Lord's purpose is to pre-sent a glorious church void of spots, wrinkles, and blemishes; one that is holy. Verse 4 tells us how Zion is purged. *Zion is purged or washed by the spirit of judgment and by the spirit of burning.* Before I began studying this, I didn't even know that there was a spirit of judgment. We see clearly through these scriptures that the spirit of judgment was loosed on Israel for the intent of excellent fruit bearing. Now let's talk a little about the remnant.

The Remnant

God sends judgment to distinguish His people; it's his call for a remnant. A remnant is defined as a part, a member, or trace re-maining. In order words, <u>a remnant is that which is fashioned after judgment is complete.</u> During the time of judgment, some will be cut off. The remnant are those who remember the Lord and know that He alone is God. Ezekiel 14: 22-23 says this about the remnant.

> Yet, behold, therein shall be left a remnant that
> shall be brought forth, both sons and daughters:
> behold, they shall see come forth unto you, and ye
> shall see their doings: and ye shall be comforted
> concerning the evil that I have brought upon Jeru-
> salem, even concerning all that I have brought upon
> it.
>
> And they shall comfort you, when ye see their ways
> and their doings: and ye shall know that I have not
> done without cause all that I have done in it, saith
> the Lord God.

Their ways and their doings are the fruit. In conclusion, the Lord says that when it is over then shall we see why He did what he did, and then shall our hearts be comforted. Hallelujah!

Chapter 4

THE TRIAL

A trial is defined as the process of testing. A defendant is put on trial because of an accusation brought up against him. The Bible acclaims Satan to be the accuser of the brethren. I Peter 4:12 says:

Beloved do not think it strange concerning the fiery
 trial which is to try you as if some strange thing
  happened to you.

Peter sounds as if he's familiar with trials. He probably wrote this passage to encourage believers who were beginning to experience trials of suffering as Christians. They were being tested and tried on every hand and they didn't understand why. Obviously, the people were feeling as if was something that should not be happening. Yet, Peter says that trials should be common and not strange amongst believers.

Every believer undergoes the process of testing. I too felt that what I was going through should not be happening. *But, it was simply that I didn't know God or the scriptures.*

I Peter 1:6-7 says:

> **In this you greatly rejoice, though now for a**
> **little while, if need be, you have been grievous**
> **by various trials,**
>
> **That the genuineness of your faith, being much**
> **more precious than gold that perishes, though it**
> **is tested by fire, may be found to praise, honor,**
> **and glory at the revelation of Jesus Christ.**

The saints who once rejoiced because of their inheritance in Christ, have now become melancholy. Just as we do today, they have become grieved because now they are facing various trials. The Apostle Paul didn't say that you need more faith or that you need to walk more with God. No, he said, "This is common; you're supposed to be tested." We thought it was strange for God to tell Abraham to offer his only son. We also thought it strange for God to tell

Hosea to marry Harlot. And, again, we thought it strange to tell Jeremiah to eat dung. The Apostle Paul tells the saints that various trials came to test the genuineness of their faith and is likened unto gold tried by fire.

The Fire

Fire has been a part of the trial process for years. In the scriptures, fire always precedes judgment. Psalms 50:3 and Psalms 97:3 states, "A fire goeth before him." The Germans 400 years after the birth of Christ practiced a method of trial by fire. People accused of crimes could not always find witnesses to support their claims. Guilt or innocence was determined by ordeals. Accused parties had to walk barefoot over red hot coals. They believed that the burns of the innocent would heal in 3 days.

1 Corinthian 3: 12-13 reads:

> **Now if any man build upon this foundation gold,**
> **silver, precious stones, wood, hay, stubble;**
>
> **Every man's work shall be made manifest: for the**

> day shall declare it, because it shall try every
> man's work of what sort it is.

When we are under test, the thing we look for is ductility. God's desire is that we mature in Him where nothing can break us. His desire is that we remain focused and trust in Him. If we are easily troubled, worried, and anxious, it is an indication that we are not yet pure gold.

Ductility

To be ductile means to be stretched, drawn or hammered thin without breaking. Gold has a higher degree of ductility than silver. When the scriptures state that we will be tried like gold, it means that like gold, it means that we will be stretched, drawn, and hammered thin with the intent of not breaking. Oh, we thought everything was going to be easy since we've accepted Christ – not so! The only way to know whether the thing we call gold is real gold is to test it. It is not until you're put through the fire that the impurities began to surface. Pure gold without the impurities is soft and pliable. It is the impurities that cause gold to harden. When we are under test, the thing we look for is ductility. God's desire is that we mature in Him where nothing can break us. His desire is that we remain focused and trust in Him. If we are easily troubled, worried, and anxious, it is an indication that we are not yet pure gold.

Malleability

To be malleable means to be hammered, pounded or pressed into various shapes without breaking or returning to its original shape. The two words obviously have similar meanings, but the characteristic I want you to notice here is that <u>it cannot return its original shape</u>. What does that mean? It means that if we allow God, **He can change us in such a way that we cannot return to our old ways, our old lifestyles.** To be malleable also means to be changed, molded, trained, or adapted. We are to be like clay in the potter's hand. God's desire is that after all the hammering and all the stretching that we don't break down or fall apart or return to our old ways. Hallelujah, this is life changing news! I want you to get this. Remember to be malleable means that we cannot return to our old state or begin to do the things we used to do. In other words, once we endured the trials, the tests, we cannot return to the old man. There has been a transformation. As soon as a problem arises, we go back to our old ways. We start smoking again, we start drinking again, instead of continuing to do good. It is necessary that we allow God to purify us as gold is purified.

Fire will purify gold and silver but it will destroy the wood, the hay, and the stubble. Now I understand how a former drug-addict who had accepted the Lord and after years of serving Him can return to his former lifestyle as a drug user. When we are being tried, we are to continue to do good works and then we shall come forth as pure gold. ***The key to triumphing in this trial is endurance.***

The Bible emphasizes that trials are inevitable in a believer's life. Those who are committed to the Lord Jesus will experience trouble.

Trials Produce Patience

Now that we know that there are going to be trials in life, let's look a little further and see what is taking place in us. Romans 5:3-4 reads:

> **And not only that but we also glory in tribu-**
> **lation knowing that tribulation produces per-**
> **severance; and perseverance, character; and**
> **character, hope.**

Here Paul gives the purpose of tribulation. **Tribulation is to produce patience or perseverance.** Some translations reads, "tribulations <u>worketh</u> patience". I like the word "worketh" because that is exactly what is happening. Tribulation is at work in us producing patience. Then, patience will work us character, the nature of God. This is what Christianity is all about.

It's interesting to note that Paul says we glory or rejoice in suffering because we know it's going to produce patience. How many of us know that we cannot obtain the promises of God without patience? The word "suffering" can refer to all kinds of trials. This includes such things as financial pressures, physical ailments and sickness, difficult circumstances, loneliness, persecution, or mistreatment. In the midst of these trials, God's producing patience in us.

Patience Produces Character

The purpose of perseverance is to produce character. We are highly gifted and anointed, but we exemplify very little godly character. Character is the pattern of behavior or personality found in an individual or group. Godly character is the attribute of God that is revealed in us. The fruits of the Spirit are the attributes of the Father that should be coming to maturity in us. When we accept Christ, He gives us His character, the fruits of the Spirit, but they are in seed form and must be developed.
Character is only developed under pressure.

Some translations use the word experience instead of character. The word experience here means trustworthiness. The Lord never changes; He is predictable, His character is trustworthy. What part of our character is trustworthy?

As a Design/Test Engineer, the only way that I can determine if my product is good is by vigorous testing. If the product passes the test over and over again, then, and only then, do I know that it is trustworthy. The part of our character that is trustworthy is our true character.

Character Produces Hope

The purpose of character is to produce hope. Hebrew 6:19 says:

> **Which hope we have as an anchor of the soul,**
> **both sure and stedfast, and which entereth**
> **into the veil;**

Hope is the anchor of our soul. An anchor is a device that holds something else secure. The anchor keeps us. Like the anchor of a ship, it keeps us from drifting away. If you lose hope, you're gone. Hope keeps us in faith. *Judgment is the process of testing that anchors us.* It is how we get rooted and grounded in the Word. I Peter 5:10 says:

> **And after you have suffered for a little while,**
> **the God of all grace, who called you to His**
> **eternal glory in Christ, will Himself perfect,**
> **strengthen, and establish you.**

Notice that none of these things will happen until after we have suffered a little while. ***Through suffering, God perfects, confirms, strengthens, and establishes us in holiness.***

>Now, let's see what brother James has to say.

James 1: 2-4 reads:

>**My brethren count it all joy when ye fall into**
>**divers temptations;**

>**Knowing this, that trying of your faith worketh**
>**patience.**

>**But let patience have her perfect work, that ye**
>**may be perfect and entire, wanting nothing.**

Brother James says to count or consider it joy when you're going through various trials. Notice verse 2 says that **when, not if,** you're going through temptations, there's something you need to know. What you need to know is that the trying of your faith worketh patience. If you don't have a reason to endure or "go through", it is hard!

When you're being tested or experiencing various trials, you began to question everything. What did I do wrong? Every time a believer falls with sickness or financial difficulty most believers think it's because of sin. Not necessarily so. It could just be the trying of their faith. The Living Bible says it this way: **Our faith can only reach full maturity when faced with difficulties and opposition.**

In these last years, I've seen many who were once believers turn back. In every case, they were going through a fiery trial unlike they had ever experienced. They didn't realize that the test precedes the promotion. If they had only endured! The Bible talks of Jesus being the author and finisher of or faith, but what most believers don't realize is that *in between the authoring and finishing of our faith is the testing of our faith.* Once again, there is no way I would release a product without putting it through rigorous testing. I test my designs over and over and over before I stamp it approved. For some reason or another, a great number of believers believe that we don't have to go through anything; that we can confess a good word and be on our merry way. Well, the Apostle Paul didn't say to stand because he ran out of words. No, he knew that we were going to be pressed on every side, and that all that would be left to do is to stand, to endure. Let's look at another example. Deuteronomy 8:2 reads:

> **Remember how the Lord your God led you all the**
> **way in the desert these forty years, to humble**
> **you and to test you in order to know what was in**
> **your heart, whether or not you would keep his**
> **commands.**

The writer said to remember that the Lord <u>led</u> you into the wilderness **to humble you, to test you, and to see what was in your heart.** The test comes to see if we will do the Word under contrary circum-stances. During the testing process, all kinds of character flaws are exposed. The test reveals what is in the heart. I use to read this scripture thinking that God was trying to see what was in my heart, but lately I've come to think differently. John 2:24-25 says:

> **But Jesus did not commit himself unto them,**

>because he knew all men.

>And needed not that any should testify of man;
>for he knew what was in man.

Jesus didn't need anyone to testify of man because he knew what was in man. When I design a product, I know the potential of that product. I know all the parts and their functions. I'm the creator of it. I believe that God wants us to see what is in our hearts; He already knows. When the pressure is on a whole lot of junk comes out of us that we didn't even know was there. Like the man born blind, judgment allows us to see. When you see what's in your heart, you're the one left with a testimony. You'll testify of the work of God in your life. For without a test, you cannot have a testimony. In Ecclesiastes 3:18 Solomon, one of the wisest men who ever lived, concluded the matter by saying:

>I said to myself concerning the sons of men,
>God has surely tested them in order for them
>>to see that they are but beast.

Now let's return back to the passage in Deuteronomy 8:2. Notice the writer says that you were **led** in the wilderness to be tested.
Now, I know that many people question whether God really test the righteous, those in right standing with Him. Well, I believe that the scriptures bear witness that He does indeed test the righteous.

The Testing Of the Righteous

Psalms 11:5 reads:

> **The Lord trieth the righteous; but the wicked and him that loveth violence his soul hateth.**

There it is in black and white. The Lord does indeed test the righteous. Genesis 22 testifies that the time came when God tested Abraham. We know that our faith is tried and that the Lord allows us to see our hearts, but what else is being tried? Jeremiah 17:9-10 reads:

> **The heart is deceitful above all things, and desperately wicked who can know it?**

> I the Lord search the heart, <u>I try the reins</u>,
> even to give everyman according to the fruit of
> his doings.

The Lord searches and tries so that he can give to every man ac-cording to his doing. What the Lord tries is not only our faith but **He tries the reins.** The word "reins' is defined as the seat of the passions and emotions, the region of the kidneys, the inmost mind, the loins (the generative organs, the pubic organs). I believe that the heart is expressed or revealed through the reins.

Love, joy, and hate are all emotions. When we are under a test, what comes forth? - The fruits of the Spirit or the fruits of our fleshly nature? Is it love or hate? -Anger or joy? - Strife or peace?

Originally, the word passion meant suffering or agony. Naturally, this reminded me of the agony and suffering of Jesus during the Crucifixion. Passion is also defined as a strong emotion that has an overcoming or compelling effect like our sexual drive or desire. Let's look, for example, at King David who fell into adultery when he was driven by lust. But first let me stop here to ask a few questions. What did God mean when He said that David could not build the temple because he was a man of war? Didn't God anoint David to be king? And, wasn't it a common practice for kings to lead war? Of, course. So what was God really saying? Couldn't God had given him rest from his enemies as he did Solomon? I wonder if he was denied because of his murderous act against Uriah? I know that many say that David's murderous act had nothing to do with the Lord denying him the privilege to build the temple. They also say that it just wasn't God's time. Well, I agree with that to a certain degree. <u>One who is learned in the scriptures know that every purpose of God is affected by both time and judgment</u>. Yes, God's decision had to do with time but it also was a judgment call. Viewing II Samuel 11:1, you'll find that the time in which King David committed adultery with Bathsheba he should have been at war. Yes, he missed it; he should have been performing his kingly duties. When we are out of order, it is quite hard to uphold the standards of God. Now I see how some of our great leaders fall into sexual sins – **our passion and emotions are tried.** <u>David's reins were</u>

tried. ***Our spirituality is directly proportional to our sexuality.*** In other words, if we can't control our sexual appetites, then we're not very spiritual.

Moses, another one of our great leaders, was so consumed with fury that he murdered an Egyptian. Again, Moses was so angry that it caused him to sin. While at Kadesh the Lord instructed Moses and Aaron <u>to speak</u> to the rock and water would come out. But, Moses was so angry with the murmuring of the congregation that <u>he smote</u> the rock twice with the rod of God. God reprimanded Moses and Aaron, and Moses was rejected and banned from leading the congregation into the promise land. Think about it. This issue was so vital to God that Moses could not finish his course. <u>Moses reins were tried</u>. ***Our spirituality is directly proportional to how well we control our tempers.*** In other words, if we can't control our tempers, we aren't very spiritual. God help me! I don't know about you but I need God to work in me. Some people think that prophesying, casting out devils, and healing the sick are the deep things of God, but I want to challenge them and say that controlling our tempers and abstaining from freshly lust are some of the deeper works of God.

The only way to avoid evil behavior is to partake of the nature of God, to partake of suffering. Suffering has always been a part of the life process. Before a woman brings forth a child into the world, she undergoes relentless pain and anguish. She must experience the pangs of suffering.

Proverbs 24:10 says:

If thou faint in the day of adversity, thy
　　strength is small.

Adversity will reveal who you are. In other words, you are weak if you can't stand the pressure of adversity.

Isaiah 30: 20 says:

And though the Lord give you the bread of afflict-
　　tion, yet shall not thy teachers be removed into a
　　corner any more, but thine eyes shall see thy
　　teachers.

Notice it was the Lord who allowed us to be fed with the bread of affliction. The teacher is present because there is something to be learned in the time of adversity. The Lord instructs us in judgment. Now, what is it that is learned? Jesus told the saints at Ephesus that "you have not so learned Christ," … It causes us to learn obedience.

Let's view Hebrews 12: 5-13. This passage reveals God's way of corrective pruning mentioned in chapter 2. However, whether it is corrective or maintenance pruning, both feel the same to the flesh.

Verse 5 says that we have forgotten the **EXHORTATION**. Now, what is the exhortation? Well, there it is in verse 5b & 6." Despise not the chastening of the Lord…" I know that doesn't sound like an exhortation but there it is. **Verse 7 states that chastening is how God deals with his own.** Verse 8 tells us that ALL are partakers of chastening. Verse 10 tells us that the purpose of chastening is that we may be partakers of his holiness. Verse 11 tells us that judgment produces the fruits of righteousness in those who are trained by it. Do you see that? Judgment trains you. You say that you want to mature in the things of God, well, this is the process. Now, verse 12 reveals my purpose in writing this book. " **To** strengthen the hands that hang down and the feeble knees, to make straight paths for their feet so that which is lame may not be dislocated, but rather be healed."

Chapter 5

DURATION OF THE TRIAL

Now that we know that we will face various trials, is there any indication as to know how long it will last? Good question? We know that in our natural court system trials can go on for very extensive lengths of time. However, let's look at the account of the children of Israel in the wilderness. The scriptures tell us that they wondered through the wilderness for 40 years. Hebrew 3:19 says that they wondered so long because of their disbelief. The children of Israel remained in their mess longer because they murmured and complained.

Deuteronomy 1:2 states that the journey from Horeb at Mt. Sinai to Kadesh-Barnea took about eleven days. From viewing the maps, it appeared to me that from Horeb to Kadesh-Barea was almost the whole journey. There-fore, under more positive circumstances, the journey would have taken roughly eleven days. What I'm trying to say is that **God did not intend for the Israelites to wonder around the desert for 40 years.** Hallelujah!

II Corinthians 4:17 reads:

> **For our light affliction which is but a moment,**
> **is working for us a more exceeding and external**
> **weight of glory**

First let me reiterate this one thing. Notice this passage says that *our light affliction is working for us*. Yes, <u>our light affliction is working for us, not against us.</u> Now obviously, in this verse the word I want you to notice is "moment". The affliction was only meant to be temporal, for a set time, subject to change, a moment.

Isaiah 54:7-8 says:

> **For a mere <u>moment</u> I have forsaken you, but with**
> **great mercies I will gather you.**
>
> **With a little wrath, I have hid my face from you**
> **for a <u>moment</u>.**
> **But with everlasting kindness I will have mercy**
> **on you says the Lord your redeemer.**

Forsaken is exactly how you fell when you are going through a hard time. You feel like you are all alone. Yet, the Lord says that it is only for a moment. When King Hezekiah was tested by the Lord, 2 Chronicles 32:31 says,

> **Howbeit in the business of the ambassadors of**
> **the princes of Babylon, who sent unto him to**
> **enquire of the wonder that was done in the land,**
> **<u>God left him, to try him,</u> that he might know all**
> **that was in his heart.**

I hope you get this. It states that "God left him to try him". God steps back and allows the enemy to do what he wills. God knows that we have everything we need in us to be more than conquerors.

Now let's look at something interesting. II Peter 3:8 says:

> **But do not let this fact escape your notice,**
> **beloved, that with the Lord one day is as a**
> **thousand years, and a thousand years is as a day.**

The Lord obviously doesn't count time as we do. When I read this, I was trying to think like God thinks so I made myself a chart. If a thousand years is as a day, then what is a moment as? I love mathematical stuff so using the relationship that a day is as a thousand years as a reference, I determined what a moment might possibly be to the lord. From the chart, if a thousand years is as a day, then I concluded that **a moment is as four days.** Of course this figure comes from a chart I made, but what I want you to see is the concept. God did not intend for us to be in the time of testing all the time. All God needs is a moment. <u>If we can just yield to God for that one moment, without the murmuring and complaining, we can be changed.</u> We do know that God has a time determined. Ecclesiastes 3:1 says:

**To everything there is a season, and a time to
every purpose under the heaven;**

Just as we came into the world at a set time, God has a set time foe every man's judgment.

Let's briefly look at the number four in scripture because it does appear to have some significance. It has been said that every man has four faces: the one he shows, the one that is seen, the one he believes to be true, and the one that is true.

In the Book of Judges, chapter 11, we are told about the story of Jephthah and how he made a vow to God. "If you will indeed deliver the people of Ammon into my hands, then it will be whatever comes out of the doors of my house to meet me when I return in peace from the people of Ammon shall surely be the Lord's, and I will sacrifice it as a burnt offering." Verse 40, tells us that from that incident came the Israelite custom. Each year the young women of Isreal would go out for four days and commemorate the daughter of Jephthah, the Gildeadite. Why four days?

The bible talks of the four winged creatures, the four winds of the earth, the four great beasts with four heads, losing the four angels, the four horns, and the four carpenters, and **<u>Lazarus laying in the tomb for four days.</u>** I believe this last one shook me. Why was Lazarus in the tomb four days? Why not 1, 2, 3, or even 7 days? When Mary called for Jesus, he purposely stayed where he was for two more days. And then there are the derivatives of the number four – the twenty four elders, the one hundred and forty four thousand, fasting for forty days and forty nights, four hundred years of captivity, and so forth.

    I can't tell you how long your trial is going to be, but I will encourage you to let it be. James says to let patience have its perfect work in you. I believe there would be no Ishmael if Abraham had let patience complete its work in him. The children of Israel would not have traveled in circles if they had not murmured against the working of God. We must allow patience to complete its work in us. Only then will we be mature and complete, lacking nothing.

    I heard a minister once say that <u>the number four is the number of qualification</u>. If this is true, which I believe it is. God is trying to tell us something. We saw earlier that we cannot qualify until after we have suffered a while. We have to be put in the fire and tried until we are pure gold.

Chapter 6

TESTIMONIALS

I must warn you that this chapter will not be what you think.
When Satan appeared before God, God began to testify about Job. For years I thought it was the other way around. Job 1:8 reads:

> And the Lord said unto Satan, hast thou considered
> my servant Job, that there is none like him in the
> Earth, a perfect and an upright man, one who feareth
> God, and escheweth evil?

What do you think? It sounds like God started all your mess. The Lord gave Satan permission to try Job. Now see yourself as the one being tried. Job 1:12 says:

> And the Lord said unto Satan, Behold, he is in
> thine hand; but save his life.

Now, if the Lord gave me permission to do whatsoever I desired, except murder, to mine enemies, what would I do? Well, I feel like it would be wise to plead the fifth. I think you get the picture. I said all that to ask this: What has the Lord testified of you? Well I believe he said something like this:

> **Go ahead and afflict their bodies, they'll still praise me.**
>
> **Go ahead and attack their sons and daughters, they'll still praise me.**
>
> **Go ahead and spoil their goods, they'll still praise me.**
>
> **Go ahead and mock them, they'll still praise me.**

The Apostle Paul exclaimed that nothing shall separate us from the love of God— not tribulation, distress, persecution, famine, naked- ness, peril, sword, death, life, angels, principles, nor powers. What is your persuasion?

Chapter 7

The Verdict

The word "verdict" is defined as the unanimous finding of a jury on the matter submitted to them in a trial. The verdict is expressed in Roman 8:18 which reads as follows:

For I reckon that the sufferings of this present
    time are not worthy to be compared to the glory
    that shall be revealed in us.

The conclusion of the matter is that this present suffering, this present judgment, is not worthy to be compared to the glory that shall be revealed in us. There is nothing that we go through that can compare to the glory that shall be revealed. If we don't partake of the suffering, we will not partake of the glory.

Hebrews 5:8&9:

Though He was a Son yet He learned obedience by the
    things which he suffered and having perfected, He

> became the author of eternal salvation to all who obey Him.

Jesus became obedient by the things which he suffered. Verse 9 says, "And having being perfected..." He was perfected when he learned obedience through suffering. Likewise, **we will never be perfected until we become obedient through suffering.** Anyone can do the right thing when there are no opposing factors. The challenge comes when we are faced with opposition.

Let's Go On To Maturity

The word "perfect" here means to be thoroughly prepared or matured for every good work. Maturity is what we need to press toward; it's our desired end. The word "mature" means to bring full growth or development, to cause or ripen. God has designed a process by which fruit grows and in a like manner He has designed a process by which Christians grow spiritually. Hebrew 5:13-14 says:

> For everyone the useth milk is unskillful in the word
> of righteousness: for he is a babe. But strong meat be-

>longeth to them that are full age, even those who by
>reason of use have their senses exercised to discern
>both good and evil.

Here the one of full age refers to him who is mature or perfect. The word "discern" here means to separate, to judge, to determine, and to decide. The process of discerning between good and evil is judgment. <u>The only way one's senses are exercised is to be faced with both good and evil.</u> Those who are babes in the Lord lack the spiritual sensitivity to distinguish good from evil. The mature saint, on the other hand, practices the word. The practice exercises in a textbook are there to prepare us for every test of life.

The word "perfect" also means to restore. Everything Job lost was restored back to him. I think it's interesting to note that God even gave Job ten more children. He also received twice as much cattle, gold, and silver. Natural things lost in the time of judg-ment shall be restored, but most importantly one will have uncovered a treasure of spiritual wealth.

The Glory Revealed In Us

The earlier passage we read states that "the glory shall be revealed in us." I am convinced that God put something in us to expose Himself. Roman 8:19 reads:

For the earnest expectation of the creature
waiteth for the manifestation of the sons of God.

This passage indicates that the true sons of God have not been revealed. Our eyes have not behold the true sons of God. ***The true sons don't surface until after the suffering, after the fire, after the trial.*** The truth of the matter is that <u>until judgment takes place, the true sons cannot be revealed.</u> In other words, I don't know who you are yet. The whole creation, animate and inanimate, is awaiting the revealing of the sons of God.

Jeremiah 29:11 states:

I know the thoughts I think towards you said
the Lord, thoughts of peace and not evil, to
give you a future and a hope.

The trials and persecutions that we presently face are to give us a future.

We are not "going through" because of our past, no, it is because of our future. "And a hope", we now know that hope is produced by character. Character is produced by patience, and patience is produced by tribulation.

So when you are in your time of judgment, even if you can't understand it, even if you can't find a scripture for it, know that God is divinely shaping your end. Nothing happens by chance. The word "trust" is mentioned numerous times in the Bible because it is His calling for our lives. So when you don't understand, just "trust". He is divinely orchestrating your destiny toward maturity.

www.ingramcontent.com/pod-product-compliance
Lightning Source LLC
Chambersburg PA
CBHW051956290426
44110CB00015B/2269